William Vaughan

WILLIAM BLAKE

With 46 color plates

PARK SOUTH BOOKS
An imprint of
Publishers Marketing Enterprises Inc.
386 Park Avenue South
New York, New York 10016

Published by PARK SOUTH BOOKS
An imprint of Publishers Marketing Enterprises Inc.
386 Park Avenue South
New York, New York 10016

First published in the U.K. by
Thames and Hudson Ltd, London

© John Calmann and Cooper Ltd, 1977
This book was designed and produced by
John Calmann and Cooper Ltd, London

Reprinted 1985

Library of Congress Catalog Card Number: 84–61597

ISBN 0–917923–01–4

Printed in Hong Kong by Mandarin Offset Ltd

Introduction

IT IS A HUNDRED AND FIFTY YEARS since William Blake died, and yet he is still a controversial figure. For this English poet and artist is so extreme in his assertions, so inspired and yet so naïve in his art, that he cuts across all conventional means of assessment. It is true that his emergence is less of a mystery to us than it was to earlier generations. A wealth of scholarship in recent decades has shown that his prophetic claims had many parallels in the unsettled times in which he lived, rent as they were by those political and social crises epitomized by the French Revolution of 1789. Furthermore the heroic and primitive tendencies in his art can now be seen to be closely related to the preoccupations of other, more conventional artists of the day. Yet the synthesis he made from these is unique and there is no confusing his works with those of any of his contemporaries.

The most striking feature of Blake's art is its visionary character. He was a 'seer' in the literal sense of the word, for whom the realm of the spirit was every bit as tangible as the material world. Nor did this power seem incidental to his creative gifts; indeed, he felt that it was only through artistic intuition that the deeper reality could be perceived – a reflection that led him to describe Jesus Christ and all true spiritual leaders as 'artists'. His own talents were wide-ranging. He was equally gifted as a poet and a painter, and is reputed to have composed fine music as well. It is in fact hard to view his pictorial work in isolation. It was continuously fired by the written word, by the Bible, Dante, the great English poets and by his own writings. Despite this his pictures are not 'literary' in the sense of being merely illustrative. He was too much a master of both word and image to make one do the job of the other. The link between his activities reached to a more fundamental level, to that rhythmic intensity which can be found in all great poetry, painting and music. While Blake sometimes showed shortcomings in such learnable pictorial skills as anatomy and perspective, his art is sustained throughout by the vibrancy of its line. It is this which gives vigour to such monumental works as *Nebuchadnezzar* (*plate 13*) and which enlivens the lyricism of the gentlest moments in the *Songs of Innocence* (*plate 4*).

In contrast to the wealth of his inner life, Blake's material existence was a modest one. The son of a hosier, he was born in London on 28th November 1757. Throughout his seventy years of life he was poor and, with the exception of three years in the country between 1800 and 1803, never moved away from his native city. While his artistic intentions were not discouraged by his family, they were turned to practical use. In 1772 he was apprenticed to the reproductive engraver James Basire, with whom he remained for the customary seven years. This training was important for providing him with a means of livelihood which he was to fall back on throughout his career. As well as this it gave him that knowledge of engraving processes which was to be put to such good use when he was evolving his own printing methods for his illuminated books in the late 1780s.

Perhaps Basire's instruction also encouraged Blake's interest in linear precision. For the engraver was a meticulous if somewhat pedestrian craftsman who specialized in topographical and antiquarian work. However, the taste for clear outline was also one that accorded with the mounting severity of the contemporary classical revival. It was this style that Blake emulated when he set out, at the end of his apprenticeship, to establish a reputation as an artist in his own right.

As part of this ambition he enrolled at the Royal Academy Schools in 1779. Although his stay there was not long, it did bring him into contact with a number of promising young artists. In particular he became friendly with John Flaxman, the Neo-classical sculptor who was to become famous throughout Europe fifteen years later for his outline drawings of scenes from Homer and Dante. Between 1780 and 1785 Blake exhibited a number of historical and religious designs at the Royal Academy, and those that survive (*plate 1*) show an emphasis on contour and compositional clarity that has affinities with the works of such notable Neo-classical artists of the day as James Barry and Benjamin West.

In these early years Blake's imaginative powers were already attracting interest in certain artistic and intellectual circles. Indeed some admirers, including Flaxman, clubbed together to pay for the printing of a book of Blake's writings, the *Poetical Sketches* in 1783, although the work was never actually published. However, his professional prospects remained uncertain. An engraving business that he set up in 1784 was disbanded in the following year. In 1785, too, the carefully worked up watercolours that he sent to the Royal Academy (*plate 1*) were harshly criticized by the President, Sir Joshua Reynolds. Blake was not to exhibit his work again for fourteen years and even then, he did so infrequently.

Such setbacks, which were no doubt harder to bear now that he had a wife to support (he had married in 1782), seem to have thrown Blake increasingly upon his inner resources. With his growing independence of thought and action there came that marked opposition to authoritarianism that was to characterize his subsequent publications. He certainly sympathized with the radical extremists of the time, and became acquainted in 1788 with such social reformers as the republican Tom Paine – soon to be driven from England for his support of the French Revolution – and the defender of women's rights, Mary Wollstonecraft. At the same time he became more extreme in his pictorial art, showing an appreciation of the dramatic productions of the recently deceased John Hamilton Mortimer, and of the bizarre expressionistic paintings of his older contemporary Henry Fuseli.

Blake's individualism culminated in his decision to address the public directly, without the intermediary of either Academy or publisher, by producing books which he wrote, designed, and printed himself. The result was a remarkable series of illustrated texts which appeared over a span of thirty odd years. These contained the body of Blake's thought and much of his most potent imagery.

The method that Blake used to produce these represented something of a technical breakthrough for it enabled text and illustration to be designed and printed on a single plate. Characteristically he claimed that it had been revealed to him in vision by the spirit of his favourite brother Robert, whose death in 1787 had moved him so deeply. Basically the process involved drawing and writing on a metal plate with an acid-resistant gum. The plate was then placed in a bath of acid so that the uncovered areas were eaten away, leaving the inscribed parts in relief. It was from these raised sections that the impression was taken. Although difficult to carry out, the method involved no elaborate machinery and could be practiced by Blake in his own home. After printing, each page would be hand-coloured by himself or his wife. Every copy of every book, therefore, was unique.

The first work in which this process was successfully used was the *Songs of Innocence* (1789) (*plate 4*). A delightfully decorated collection of short lyrical poems, it seems remarkably innocuous in content. It is true that it placed more emphasis on emotion than reason, but it did not attack the conventions of the age in the way that Blake's later works were to do. Very different is the book's sequel, the *Songs of Experience* (1793) which are concerned with human misery and corruption. Perhaps the change was precipitated by a worsening in the artist's own position. Like many radicals he suffered from the reactionary backlash in England that followed on the revolutionary events in France. In the autumn of 1790 he moved away from the centre of London to the relative isolation of Lambeth, where he was to remain until 1800.

It was from Lambeth that the great 'prophetic' books of the 1790s were issued. Their mood was preluded by the satirical *Marriage of Heaven and Hell* (1790) (*plate 6*), in which he contested the views of one of his former mentors, the Swedish divine Emanuel Swedenborg. Finding the conventional division of good and evil that Swedenborg supported to be repressive, Blake concentrated on those positive values that had been proscribed by being thought wicked. Much of the book is given over to 'Proverbs of Hell', which include such arresting libertarian pronouncements as 'The road of excess leads to the palace of wisdom', 'Exuberance is beauty' and 'One Law for the Lion and Ox is oppression'.

The 'prophetic' books themselves were larger both in scope and format. Like one of the prophets of the Old Testament, Blake set out in these to expose human errors and indicate the true path. He took his cue from the most pressing problems of the day – rebellion in the New World (*America*, 1793), revolution in the old (*Europe*, 1794 (*plates 8 and 9*), sexual repression and other forms of slavery (*Visions of the Daughters of Albion*, 1793 (*plate 7*)). The final book, *Jerusalem* (1804–20), reviews the whole history of man, showing the misery caused by his limited spiritual vision, and predicting his salvation and ultimate union with eternity. It is not hard to see why Blake should have felt drawn to undertake such an ambitious programme – especially when Europe was undergoing such turmoil. But it does seem strange at first that he should have chosen to cast his prophecies in the form of mythological sagas peopled with such obscurely named characters as the innocent Oothon or the harsh deity Urizen.

Certainly he was not being esoteric, for although his books were bought by no more than a handful of faithful friends and collectors of curios they were clearly intended for a wide public. The reason seems to lie rather in his appreciation of the nature of myth itself. Blake shared the growing fascination of his age with the legends of the ancient world which he saw as creative and imaginative accounts of the fundamentals of existence. While not true in a prosaic sense, they contain insights into a reality that no rational process could reach. Blake's own mythology is dramatic and inspired. The qualities it embodies are not directly translatable, and any attempt to do so must reduce it to aridity and lifelessness. His deeper meaning is not to be illuminated by minute exegesis, but only by a corresponding leap in our own imaginations.

In these books the relief etching technique reached new heights of perfection. At times the imagery flows around the words, at times it is quite independent, sometimes even in subject matter. Blake was an heir to the Neo-Platonic notion that pictorial images were an essential means of communicating the ideal. He believed that they provided insights equal, if not superior, in value to those of words. He therefore took as much trouble to emulate the qualities of the art of the ancient world, as he did to imitate its myths and prophecies. He even assumed a biblical precedent for such work, following a belief current at the time that the statues of Greece and the hieroglyphs of Egypt were derived from a lost Hebrew art.

The importance that Blake gave to archetypal imagery is borne out by the series of twelve large prints that he produced between about 1794 and 1796. As with his illuminated books, these involved the invention of a new process. In this case impressions were taken from a painted-up board. Such 'monoprints' (each board, in fact, yielded a maximum of three prints) were then touched up with pen and watercolour. Many of the forms in these plates were taken from Blake's books and like the book illustrations, the 'monoprints', are critical in tone, describing the limitations of rationalism and the slavery caused by organized religion and society (*plates 11–15*). However the pictures also show a concern for succinct monumental forms of a more severe kind than those used in the historical compositions of the 1780s. Blake's admiration of the sublime grandeur of Michelangelo now had a more positive effect on his art. Indeed, some of the figures in these prints, such as *Newton* (*plate 12*), were directly copied from the work of the great Italian master.

Although Blake was an isolated figure at this time, he was far from being completely overlooked. His standing was still sufficiently high for him to receive important commercial commissions, such as the decoration of the popular poet Edward Young's *Night Thoughts* with 537 rich border illustrations. Only part of this ambitious project was actually published (in 1796), but it did lead to a further private one of a similar nature; the decoration of the equally fashionable poems of Thomas Gray for Flaxman's wife. Although Blake had been in sympathy with such sentimental 'graveyard' poets in his youth, he now found them mediocre, and was often critical of their powers in his surrounding illustrations. However, he was also able to enter into the spirit of the occasion, and often gave such designs a light-hearted, lyrical tone that contrasts strongly with the grimmer mood of his own themes.

After 1800 such lyricism took on a more positive value in his art. He now emphasized the ecstatic side of his vision, the contemplation of the Divine. It was an auspicious time for him, in which new benefactors emerged. Between 1800 and 1803 one of these, the gentleman poet William Hayley, accommodated him in a cottage in the country, at Felpham, Sussex. More important, however, was the minor civil servant Thomas Butts whom Blake described as the 'angel to my visions'. Though not a wealthy man, Butts was to be the artist's principal patron (at times, indeed, his only one) for the next two decades.

The first commission that Butts gave Blake – in 1799 – was for a series of biblical scenes. These the artist executed in a form of tempera painting. He preferred this archaic technique to the more usual one of oil, for he saw the latter, with its capacity for rich tonalities, as the medium that favoured the soft, sensual art of such 'materialists' as the Venetian painters or Rubens. Tempera, which he confused with the fresco wall-painting of the early Italian masters, seemed to him to avoid all facile effects and encourage instead the clear designs and firm contours of his own inspired art. It was some years, however, before he fully mastered this technique, and his early tempera paintings now appear dim and murky.

Meanwhile his most effective paintings were executed in watercolour; a technique that also favours linearity even if it does lack the density of tempera. It was in watercolour that Blake executed a second series of biblical scenes for Butts (*plates 16–19*). These pictures show that Blake was now looking at mediaeval art with new attentiveness. Ever since he had been sent as an apprentice to make drawings from the Royal Tombs in Westminster Abbey he had had an admiration for gothic: and, indeed, his illuminated books have their closest parallel in the manuscripts of the middle ages. Now, however, he emulated the actual style of gothic, the attenuated forms and ethereal effects. It is significant that he should at this time have turned his back on Greek art, dismissing its measured forms as 'mathematical'. Gothic, by contrast, was a 'living form'.

At times there are direct copies of mediaeval figures in these watercolours. There is also a general symmetrical tendency in their design which is reminiscent of the hieratic form of early altarpieces and emphasizes Blake's view of painting as a religious act. Perhaps the most striking feature of these works, however, is their gentle radiance which gives these devotional works such visionary quality. These characteristics were to be sustained in the themes from Milton that Blake subsequently painted for Butts. Here, however, the effects were supplemented by a richer range of colours (*plates 25–26*).

Despite the general lack of interest in his productions, Blake still dreamed of coming before the public and even of executing major monumental works like his beloved Michelangelo and the religious artists before him. It was this hope that spurred him, in 1809, to mount a one-man show in his brother's house off Golden Square in Soho. The exhibition, which contained many designs the artist would like to have executed on a monumental scale, was up for over a year, but it was a complete failure. The only paper to review it, *The Examiner*, dismissed the whole business as a 'farago of nonsense' and none of the works were sold. Only one visitor viewed it sympathetically. This was the lawyer Henry Crabb Robinson who had a close knowledge of the works of the German Romantics, and who found interesting comparisons between their outlook and that of Blake.

The years that followed Blake's exhibition were his most obscure. He received only the most menial of commercial commissions, and had more difficulty than ever in selling his original works. Even the enthusiasm of Thomas Butts dwindled. Yet curiously none of this seems to have affected the mood of his art. He continued steadfastly with his great apocalyptic work, *Jerusalem* and with the production of Miltonic watercolours.

Around 1818 Blake's fortunes began to improve. Now over sixty, he was taken up by a much younger generation who, under the influence of the growing Romantic movement, took a sympathetic view of the artist who opposed rationalism, was guided by visions and admired the primitive. The most important of these was the painter John Linnell. A shrewd businessman, Linnell provided Blake with rewarding employment; it was through his offices that Blake was commissioned to provide wood-engravings for a school edition of Virgil's *Eclogues* (*The Pastorals of Virgil*, 1821). While the vigour of these horrified the editor, Dr. Robert Thornton, they were received with great enthusiasm by the artist's friends. The vividness of the rural scenes they described was to be immensely influential on the landscapes of one of these, the young Samuel Palmer who, for a time, worked with a group of associates styled 'the Ancients' in the Kent village of Shoreham, depicting the local scenery with Blakean fervour. Another project instigated by Linnell, the engraving of Blake's *Illustration of the Book of Job* (1825), also contains much pastoral imagery. One of the few works by Blake that was genuinely popular during his lifetime, it eased the artist's poverty during his last two years of life.

Blake's last major undertaking, the production of watercolours and engravings illustrating the *Divine Comedy* of Dante, was commissioned, like the *Job*, by Linnell. Unfinished at the time of his death, it shows that he was at the height of his powers right at the end of his life (*plates 34–40*). Pictures like the *Circle of the Lustful* (*plate 37*) or *The Simoniac Pope* (*plate 38*) combine a Michelangelesque vigour and Gothic sinuousness with magnificent, flickering colour effects. These evoke so vividly a sense of the unearthly regions of Hell, Purgatory and Paradise through which Dante passes in his epic poem, that it might be supposed that Blake was closely following the intentions of the author he was illustrating. Yet he had, in fact, severe reservations about the mediaeval Italian's vision, finding it too legalistic. As ever, Blake had his own point of view which he could not suppress in deference to the opinions of others.

Blake died on 12th August 1827, a few months before his seventieth birthday. His last years appear to have been tranquil, for although his worldly success had been limited, he had the satisfaction of knowing that he had remained true to his inner vision throughout the decades of privation and opposition. And in the large oeuvre that he left behind him, it is this irrepressible conviction that triumphs, making his challenging art so vigorous and exciting.

1. *Joseph Making Himself Known to his Brethren*

c.1784–5. Watercolour and ink. $15\frac{7}{8} \times 22\frac{1}{8}$ in (40·3 × 56·2cm)

One of the three large and carefully finished watercolours of the biblical story of Joseph which Blake exhibited at the Royal Academy in 1785. This one shows the moment when Joseph (the gesticulating figure on the left) reveals his true identity to his brothers and foregives them their crime against him. Executed at a time when Blake still hoped for conventional success as a painter of historical and imaginative subjects, it shows the succinct outlines and carefully controlled design favoured by contemporary Neo-classical taste.

Cambridge, Fitzwilliam Museum

2. *Oberon, Titania and Puck with Fairies Dancing*

c.1785–90. Watercolour. 18¾ × 26½ in (47·5 × 62·5 cm)

This is a lyrical rendering of the final scene of *A Midsummer Night's Dream*. On the left are Oberon and Titania. Now reconciled, they bless the state of marriage as their attendant fairies dance. While close in style to the *Story of Joseph* series (*plate 1*) the picture is looser in handling and is possibly unfinished. Shakespearian subjects were popular amongst artists and patrons in England in the late eighteenth century. Around the time Blake executed this design, his friend Henry Fuseli was painting scenes from the same play to form part of the 'Shakespeare Gallery' being assembled by the wealthy publisher Alderman Boydell.

London, Tate Gallery

3. *The Penance of Jane Shore in St. Paul's Church*

c.1790. Watercolour and pen (varnished). $9\frac{5}{8} \times 11\frac{5}{8}$ in (24·5 × 29·5cm)

Jane Shore was the mistress of Edward IV. After his death in 1483 she was condemned to do penance at St. Paul's church by the succeeding monarch, Richard III. Her beauty and bearing during her trials were reputed to have aroused much sympathy which certainly seems to be the sentiment expressed by the soldiers and onlookers in Blake's watercolour. The subject's implied criticism of conventional sexual morality accorded with the artist's own views. Blake first treated the theme around 1778–80 when designing a series of scenes from British history; however this version is normally dated around 1790 on account of its more accomplished handling.

London, Tate Gallery

4. *Songs of Innocence*

Title Page; The Shepherd; The Divine Image; Infant Joy.
First published 1789. Relief etchings with watercolour.
Approximately $4\frac{1}{2} \times 2\frac{3}{4}$ in (11·3 × 7·2cm)

This tiny volume was the first of a long line of books that Blake published using a relief-etching method of his own devising. This enabled him to achieve a close unity between each poem and the surrounding design. Often the effect is reminiscent of a mediaeval manuscript. The simple lyrics and idyllic sentiments of this work have made it the most popular of Blake's productions; it concentrates on children and the gentler aspects of the natural world and much of the imagery is pastoral. But it also has a more profound side which comes to the fore in such poems as *The Divine Image* which emphasizes the presence of the Divine in humanity.

Washington, Library of Congress

SONGS
of
Innocence

1789

The Author & Printer W Blake

The Shepherd.

How sweet is the Shepherds sweet lot!
From the morn to the evening he strays:
He shall follow his sheep all the day
And his tongue shall be filled with praise.

For he hears the lambs innocent call:
And he hears the ewes tender reply:
He is watchful while they are in peace,
For they know when their Shepherd is nigh.

The Divine Image.

To Mercy Pity Peace and Love,
All pray in their distress:
And to these virtues of delight
Return their thankfulness.

For Mercy Pity Peace and Love,
Is God our father dear:
And Mercy Pity Peace and Love,
Is Man his child and care.

For Mercy has a human heart
Pity, a human face:
And Love, the human form divine,
And Peace, the human dress.

Then every man of every clime,
That prays in his distress,
Prays to the human form divine
Love Mercy Pity Peace.

And all must love the human form,
In heathen, turk or jew
Where Mercy, Love & Pity dwell
There God is dwelling too.

Infant Joy

I have no name
I am but two days old. —
What shall I call thee?
I happy am
Joy is my name. —
Sweet joy befall thee!

Pretty joy!
Sweet joy but two days old,
Sweet joy I call thee:
Thou dost smile.
I sing the while
Sweet joy befall thee.

5. Songs of Experience

Frontispiece; The Sick Rose; The Tyger; A Poison Tree.
First published 1794. Relief etchings with watercolour. 27
pages. Approximately $4\frac{1}{2} \times 2\frac{3}{4}$ in ($11 \cdot 3 \times 7 \cdot 2$cm)

Issued as a sequel to *Songs of Innocence* (*plate 4*), which was republished with it, many of the poems in *Songs of Experience* are direct antitheses to those in the earlier work. They reflect the growing disillusion that Blake had experienced in the intervening years. As the frontispiece suggests the 'poet' shepherd now proceeds with new determination and insight. He questions the fundamental goodness of the world (*The Sick Rose*), exposes human injustice (*The Tyger*), and admits to feelings of evil and jealousy (*Poison Tree*). Once more the illustrations extend the meaning of the poems – though with more striking accomplishment. As might be expected, the colours used tend to be more sombre than in the *Songs of Innocence*.

Washington, Library of Congress

The SICK ROSE

O Rose thou art sick.
The invisible worm.
That flies in the night
In the howling storm:

Has found out thy bed
Of crimson joy:
And his dark secret love
Does thy life destroy.

The Tyger.

Tyger Tyger. burning bright,
In the forests of the night;
What immortal hand or eye.
Could frame thy fearful symmetry?

In what distant deeps or skies.
Burnt the fire of thine eyes?
On what wings dare he aspire?
What the hand, dare seize the fire?

And what shoulder, & what art,
Could twist the sinews of thy heart?
And when thy heart began to beat,
What dread hand? & what dread feet?

What the hammer? what the chain,
In what furnace was thy brain?
What the anvil? what dread grasp.
Dare its deadly terrors clasp?

When the stars threw down their spears
And water'd heaven with their tears:
Did he smile his work to see?
Did he who made the Lamb make thee?

Tyger Tyger burning bright,
In the forests of the night:
What immortal hand or eye.
Dare frame thy fearful symmetry?

A POISON TREE.

I was angry with my friend:
I told my wrath, my wrath did end.
I was angry with my foe:
I told it not, my wrath did grow.

And I waterd it in fears,
Night & morning with my tears:
And I sunned it with smiles,
And with soft deceitful wiles.

And it grew both day and night.
Till it bore an apple bright.
And my foe beheld it shine,
And he knew that it was mine.

And into my garden stole,
When the night had veild the pole;
In the morning glad I see;
My foe outstretchd beneath the tree.

6. *The Marriage of Heaven and Hell*

*c.1790–3. Relief etching with watercolour. 6 × 4¼ in
(15 × 10·5 cm)*

A prose work conceived as a critique of *Heaven and Hell*,
one of the writings of the Swedish divine Emanuel
Swedenborg whose doctrines had greatly influenced Blake
in the late 1780s. In the book Blake suggests that the
conventional distinctions of good and evil, which
Swedenborg supported, were in fact a suppression of vital
energies beneath lifeless regulations. The exuberant
imagery of the title page bears out the message of the
book. It contrasts a barren earth with the flaming Hell
beneath. It is in the latter that 'good' and 'evil' are
reunited as an angel and devil embrace in the lower
depths.

Washington, Library of Congress

7. Visions of the Daughters of Albion; The Argument

c.1794–5. Relief etching with watercolour. 6¾ × 4¾ in (17 × 12cm)

One of the earliest of Blake's illuminated 'prophetic' books, in which an invented mythology is used to attack contemporary mores. Here the target is sexual conventions and the suffering they bring to the 'Daughters of Albion', that is the women of England. *The Argument* depicts the moment when Oothon, the heroine, innocently indulges in sexual curiosity (she is shown plucking a marigold in the vale of Leutha). Subsequently she is raped and enslaved in a union that neither she nor her oppressor desires. The simplicity of this design contrasts strongly with the tortuous imagery to come.

Princeton, University Library

The Argument

I loved Theotormon
And I was not ashamed
I trembled in my virgin fears
And I hid in Leutha's vale;

I plucked Leutha's flower,
And I rose up from the vale;
But the terrible thunders tore
My virgin mantle in twain.

8. *Europe, a Prophecy; the Ancient of Days*

First published 1794. Relief etching with watercolour. c.1821.
12¼ × 9½ in (30·4 × 23·6 cm)

Both *America* and its sequel, *Europe*, deal with the
upheavals of Blake's own time. In *Europe* the troubles are
traced back to the misunderstanding of the true message
of Christianity. Under the baleful influence of the harsh
law-giving deity Urizen, Europe develops a repressive and
materialistic society that eventually provokes the violent
reaction of the French Revolution. The magnificent
frontispiece shown here, one of Blake's most famous
designs, shows Urizen measuring out the material world.
Dividers, a traditional attribute of God as creator, were
frequently used by Blake as an image of soulless
construction as in *Newton* (*plate 12*).

Cambridge, Fitzwilliam Museum

9. *Europe, A Prophecy; Blighted crops*

First published 1794. Relief etching with watercolour. c.1821.
12¼ × 9½ in (30·4 × 23·6cm)

Although not illustrating an event mentioned in the text
of *Europe*, the picture represents the continent's miseries in
allegorical form. Two sprites blast the earth's produce with
seeds of destruction. This plate, like the preceding one,
come from a particularly finely coloured version of *Europe*,
which was executed for John Linnell, the most important
of Blake's patrons in his last years.

Cambridge, Fitzwilliam Museum

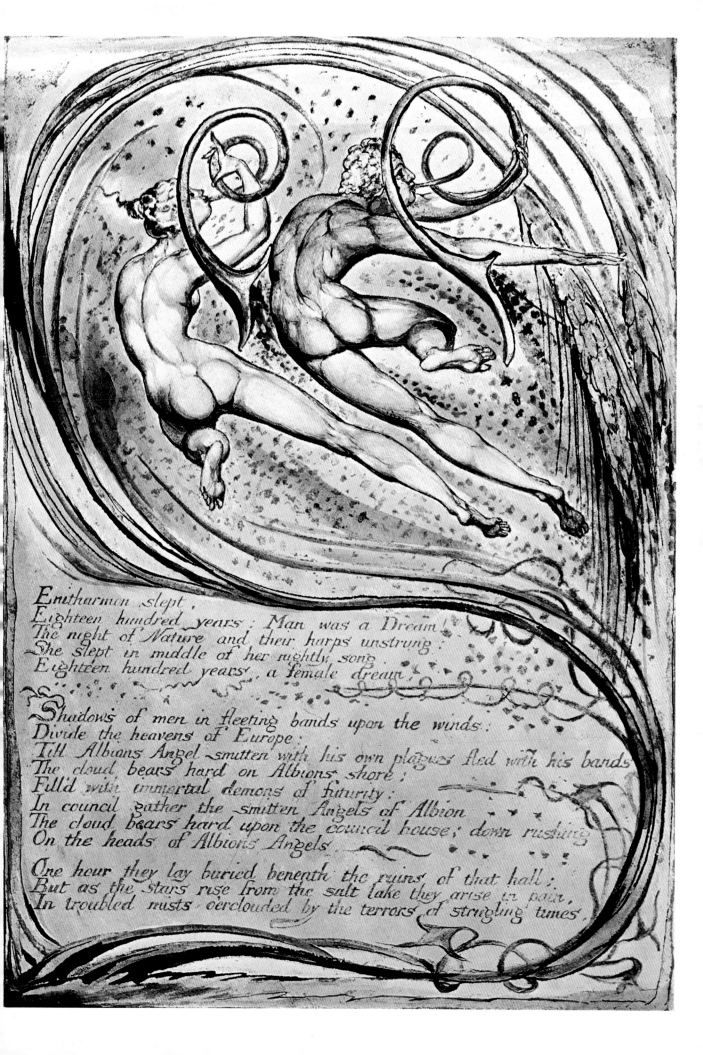

Enitharmon slept,
Eighteen hundred years; Man was a Dream!
The night of Nature and their harps unstrung:
She slept in middle of her nightly song,
Eighteen hundred years, a female dream.

Shadows of men in fleeting bands upon the winds:
Divide the heavens of Europe;
Till Albions Angel smitten with his own plagues fled with his bands
The cloud bears hard on Albions shore;
Fill'd with immortal demons of futurity:
In council gather the smitten Angels of Albion
The cloud bears hard upon the council house; down rushing
On the heads of Albions Angels.

One hour they lay buried beneath the ruins of that hall;
But as the stars rise from the salt lake they arise in pain,
In troubled mists o'erclouded by the terrors of struggling times

10. *Glad Day or The Dance of Albion*

First engraved 1780, coloured 1794–6. Engraving with watercolour. $10\frac{3}{4} \times 7\frac{1}{2}$ in (27·3 × 19·5cm)

According to an inscription on a later version of this engraving, the ecstatic figure is Albion (i.e. England) rising from bondage; his pose is taken from a diagram illustrating human proportions as conceived by the Ancient Roman architect Vitruvius. The plate may originally have been intended to form an optimistic conclusion to the series of illustrations of scenes from English history that Blake was planning between 1778 and 1780 (*plate 3*). Although this print is so heavily overpainted that the engraved lines can not be seen, other copies show the date 1780.

London, British Museum

11. *Elohim creating Adam*

c.1795. Monoprint, with pen and watercolour. $17 \times 21\frac{1}{8}$ in (42·1 × 53·6cm)

A most severe interpretation of the creation of man. Elohim is the Hebrew name for God in his aspect of justice. He is shown here as a terrifying, stone-like, figure virtually dragging the protesting form of man from the world of the spirit into the enslavement of mortality. This large design is one of a group of twelve that were executed in about 1795 (also *plates 12–15*). They represent a high point in his experimentation with colour printing. A maximum of three impressions were taken direct from a piece of millboard upon which the subject had been painted in tempera. These were subsequently touched up with pen and watercolour.

London, Tate Gallery

12. *Newton*

1795. Monoprint, with pen and watercolour. $18\frac{1}{8} \times 23\frac{5}{8}$ in (46 × 60cm)

The famous British scientist has been transposed here into an allegorical image of materialism. Using a pair of dividers, like the harsh diety Urizen in *The Ancient of Days* (*plate 9*), he imposes a rational order on the world. Like the other monoprints, this composition shows Blake's interest at this time in creating succinct, monumental forms. In this case the figure is based on Michelangelo's representation of the prophet Abias in the Sistine Chapel.

London, Tate Gallery

13. *Nebuchadnezzar*

1795. Monoprint, with pen and watercolour. $17\frac{5}{8} \times 24\frac{3}{8}$ in (44·6 × 62 cm)

An illustration to the Biblical account of the Babylonian monarch who went insane after persecuting the Jews. Blake has responded to the description in *Daniel IV* of how the king became as an animal, eating grass like oxen, his hair growing 'like eagle's feathers' and his nails 'like bird's claws'. It has been suggested that this print may have been a pendant to *Newton* (*plate 13*). Like it, it represents a man devoid of spiritual vision. It also shows a full use of the rich textures and flickering light effects that the monoprint method could produce to create a doom-laden atmosphere.

London, Tate Gallery

14. *Pity*

c.1795. Monoprint, with pen and watercolour. 16¾ × 21¼ in
(42·5 × 53·9cm)

An allegorical design apparently inspired by the lines in
Macbeth, Act One, Scene Seven, that describe pity as
   '. . . like a naked new-borne babe
  striding the blast, or Heaven's Cherubim, horsed upon
  the sightless carriers of the air.'
In *Urizen* (1794) Blake depicted Pity as a weak, divisive
force, and this attitude is borne out in this design in the
clear separation between the victim and the ethereal
onlookers. Although gentler than the other monoprints it
is, in fact, equally critical in tone.

London, Tate Gallery

15. *The Lazar House*

1795. Monoprint, with pen and watercolour. $19\frac{1}{8} \times 24in$ (48·5 × 61cm)

The scene is based on the description of a lazar house in Milton's *Paradise Lost*, *XI*, *477–493*. Diseased victims writhe in agony, presided over by Death – who looks much like Blake's harsh deity Urizen (*plate 9*). This is a particularly fresh and vigorous monoprint impression which has required very little working up with pen and water colour.

Cambridge, Fitzwilliam Museum

16. *Bathsheba at the Bath*

1799–1800. Tempera. 10½ × 14¾ in (26·3 × 37·6 cm)

One of the first series of illustrations to the Bible painted
for Thomas Butts, Blake's most important patron in the
first and second decades of the nineteenth century. The
scene is taken from *II Samuel XI, 2* and concerns the
beautiful wife of Uriah the Hittite, who was desired by
King David after this monarch had seen her taking a bath.
The two children shown with her do not occur in the
Biblical text. This series is one of the earliest examples of
Blake's use of tempera. He preferred the archaic medium
to oil, since he felt it was more austere in its effects. Despite
this, it has been used here in a sensuous manner,
presumably because of the erotic nature of the subject.

London, Tate Gallery

17. *Jacob's Ladder*

1800–03. Watercolour. $14\frac{1}{2} \times 11\frac{1}{4}$ in (36·8 × 28·9cm)

One of the finest of a series of watercolours illustrating biblical themes which Blake painted for Thomas Butts. It shows Jacob asleep at the bottom of the picture, dreaming of the ladder reaching from earth to heaven with angels ascending and descending, as described in *Genesis XXV, 12*. The striking spiral form of the 'ladder' and the inclusion of humans amongst the ascending forms emphasizes Blake's interpretation of this dream as a metaphor for the soul's aspiration to be reunited with God.

London, The British Museum

18. *God Blessing the Seventh Day*

c.1805. Watercolour. 19 × 16½in (41·9 × 35·5cm)

This biblical illustration indicates most clearly Blake's renewed interest in Gothic art. The image of God, encircled by six angels, blessing the Seventh Day at the end of the creation has been shown to be based upon a mediaeval roof boss in York Minster. The ethereal light and symmetrical arrangement are typical of this series, and contrast strongly with the dark dramatic paintings of the 1790s.

U.K., Private Collection

19. *The Great Red Dragon and the Woman Clothed with the Sun*

c.1806–9. Watercolour. 16¼ × 13½ in (42 × 34·3 cm)

The illustrations to *Revelations* form an important group in the series of biblical watercolours that Blake painted for Thomas Butts. This painting illustrates the opening verses of *Revelations XII*, which describe a 'great red dragon' waiting before 'the woman clothed with the sun' to devour the child that she is about to give birth to. According to tradition the dragon is worldly power and the woman Israel, oppressed in her innocence by the wicked.

New York, Brooklyn Museum

20. *The Last Judgement*

1808. Tempera. $19\frac{7}{8} \times 15\frac{3}{4}$ in ($47 \cdot 5 \times 38$ cm)

Blake depicted this theme many times. This version, the most complex surviving, was painted for Lady Egremont. Its programme is described in a letter from the artist to Ozias Humphreys, the man who arranged the commission. Blake did not have the orthodox Christian vision of the Last Judgement as a cataclysmic event at the end of the world, when the good will be separated from the evil and sent respectively to everlasting bliss or eternal damnation. He saw it rather as a state of mind which occurs whenever an error is recognized – either individually or collectively – and decisively cast out.

Sussex, Petworth House

21. *The Spiritual Form of Nelson Guiding Leviathan*

c.1809. Tempera on canvas. 30 × 24¾ in (76·2 × 62·5 cm)

This was exhibited with a pendant *The Spiritual Form of Pitt Guiding Behemoth* in Blake's abortive one-man show in 1809. Treating two of the leading figures in England's struggle with France, they were critical in mood as war was, in Blake's eyes, a perversion of energy. Leviathan is the great monster of the sea in the Bible and Behemoth that of the land. In this picture the hero of Trafalgar is shown as a youth holding apart the coils of Leviathan '. . . in whose wreathings are infolded the nations of the earth'.

London, Tate Gallery

22. *Adam Naming the Beasts*

1810. Tempera on Canvas. $29\frac{1}{2} \times 24\frac{1}{4}$ in (73×60cm)

One of a group of religious half-length pictures of Adam, Eve, Christ and the Virgin and Child. They were painted for his patron Thomas Butts, and may have formed part of a wall decoration. They are all painted in tempera, and their technical quality suggests that by 1810 he had begun to master this archaic medium. Like the other pictures in this series the figure is frontal and hieratic, with strongly emphasized hand gestures. Here Adam indicates the good animals of creation with his right hand, while covering the evil serpent with his left.

Glasgow, Pollock House

23. *The Canterbury Pilgrims*

c.1809. Tempera. $18\frac{1}{4} \times 53\frac{3}{4}$in (46·4 × 136·5cm)

For Blake Chaucer was, with Shakespeare and Milton, one of the three greatest English poets. He saw the mediaeval writer's *Canterbury Tales* as including 'the characters which compose all ages and nations'. In the frieze-like procession of this large painting the pilgrims are posed as a series of archetypes, ranked according to class. They are seen setting out from the Tabarde Inn, Southwark. Behind is a fine atmospheric vista which shows Blake's gift for landscape. An engraving after the work was published in 1810. It was preceded by one of a similar theme and design by Thomas Stothard which Blake considered to be a plagiarism of his painting.

Glasgow, Pollock House

24. *The Faerie Queen*

1815. Watercolour (varnished). Detail.

This picture appears to be a pendant to *Canterbury Pilgrims*, despite its later date and different medium. The figures in it mirror the movement in the earlier work, although the gestures here are most ecstatic and the sky is peopled with mythological characters. The latter fit in with the allegorical nature of Spencer's poem and provide a critique of it.

Sussex, Petworth House

25. *Adam and Eve Sleeping*

1808. Watercolour. $19\frac{1}{2} \times 15\frac{1}{2}$in (51·8 × 39·3cm)

One of the twelve illustrations to Milton's *Paradise Lost* painted for Thomas Butts. This picture shows the moment described in Book IV, 799–803, when Adam and Eve are peacefully asleep in the Garden of Eden before the Fall. They are watched over by the angels Ithuriel and Zephan who have just discovered Satan 'squat like a toad, close at the ear of Eve' tempting her in a dream.

Boston, Museum of Fine Arts

26. *Christ Placed on the Pinnacle of the Temple*

1816–18. Watercolour. $6\frac{7}{8} \times 5\frac{1}{4}$ in (16·6 × 13·3 cm)

One of twelve designs to Milton's *Paradise Regained*. They were possibly intended as a sequel to the *Paradise Lost* illustrations, but unlike these were not bought by Thomas Butts. Although equally elaborate, their draughtsmanship is less precise and their mood less intense. This picture shows Christ triumphantly revealing himself as the Son of God after having endured Satan's final temptation.

Cambridge, Fitzwilliam Museum

27. A Prophet in the Wilderness

c.1815–20. Ink and body colour. 6¼ × 4¾ in (15·9 × 11·9cm)

An unidentified subject which has been related to the *Paradise Regained* series (*plate 26*). It cannot have been intended as part of this, however, as it differs in size and medium. It has the softer handling of Blake's later years and shows the feeling for landscape that came to the fore at this time.

Cambridge, Fitzwilliam Museum

28. *The Youthful Poet Sleeping on a Bank*

c.1816–18. Watercolour. 7 × 4¾in (17·5 × 11cm)

The concluding illustration of a group of six for Milton's light-hearted early poem *L'Allegro*. They are matched by six for its counterpart, *Il Penseroso*. The poet is shown, as described by Milton, pleasantly slumbering by a 'haunted stream' on a summer's eve. The extraordinary imagery around him is based on the metaphors invoked in the concluding stanzas of the poem. They are bound together by a gentle lyrical design and soft, cheerful colouring that captures the mood of Milton's work.

New York, Pierpont Morgan Library

29. *The Ghost of a Flea*

c.1819. Tempera and gold on panel. $8\frac{7}{8} \times 6\frac{3}{8}$ in (21·4 × 16·2cm)

In October 1819 Blake made a number of drawings of manifestations of historical and imaginary personages at the instigation of John Varley, a watercolourist who liked to dabble in the occult. On one of these occasions Blake made three sketches of the *Ghost of a Flea*. Varley later recorded the artist as having said that 'all fleas were inhabited by the souls of such men as were by nature bloodthirsty to excess'. This tempera painting, which was also owned by Varley, is based on the drawings. It adds much allegorical detail, such as the pincer and cup for catching blood. The constellation behind indicates Gemini, the zodiacal sign that belonged, in Blake's opinion, to the bloodthirsty.

London, Tate Gallery

30. *Satan Going Forth from the Presence of the Lord*

c.1821. Ink and Colour washes. $5\frac{1}{4} \times 4\frac{1}{4}$ in (13·3 × 11·2cm)

One of the series of reduced drawings made from the artist's watercolour illustrations to the Book of Job (*plate 31*) which were made when he was commissioned to engrave the series by John Linnell. In the final line engravings each design had an additional margin which contained verbal and pictorial commentaries on the subject.

Cambridge, Fitzwilliam Museum

31. *Book of Job; 'When the Morning Stars Sang Together . . .'*
c.1805–10. Watercolour. 8 × 6in (19·5 × 15cm)

The Old Testament story of Job, the man who obeyed the Lord but was still beset by misfortune, fascinated Blake throughout his life. Around 1805–10 he made a series of carefully worked-up watercolours on the theme which were later to form the basis of a book of engravings (1825). This is one of the finest of the design. It shows Job's mystical awareness of the workings of the universe after the Lord (shown here in the centre) had revealed himself. This corresponds to the fourfold nature of man. The lowest section represents the flesh, where Job and his companions sit. The Sun God Apollo (middle left) represents the intellect; opposite is the moon, who stands for feeling. The choir of angels above symbolizes the spirit.

New York, Pierpont Morgan Library

32. *The Body of Abel Found by Adam and Eve*

c.1826. Tempera on panel. $12\frac{3}{4} \times 17\frac{1}{8}$ in (32·5 × 43·3cm)

This magnificent composition appears to be a later version of a work included in Blake's exhibition of 1809. It shows the high technical standard of the artist's last tempera paintings and the powerful, highly emotive colours that he favoured at that time. The blood red sun sets the mood of the tragedy. The moment depicted is not one described in the account of the murder in *Genesis*. It does, however, have affinities with passages in Salomon Gessner's *The Death of Abel* (1758), an epic poem that was highly popular at the time and much illustrated by artists.

London, Tate Gallery

33. *The Wise and Foolish Virgins*

c.1822. Pen, wash and watercolour. $14\frac{1}{2} \times 13\frac{1}{4}$in
(36·3 × 33·7cm)

An illustration of the parable told by Christ in *Matthew xxv, 1–9*. On the left are the five wise virgins, who stand with their lamps prepared in readiness for the bridegroom. They tell the lamenting and disorganized virgins on the left to go and buy the oil for their empty lamps from 'them that sell'. Above them a trumpeting angel heralds the approach of the bridegroom. Blake painted six versions of this subject. This one was probably executed for John Linnell.

Cambridge, Fitzwilliam Museum

34. *Dante Running from the Wild Beasts*

c.1824–6. Watercolour. 14¼ × 20in (36·5 × 52cm)

His illustrations to Dante's *Divine Comedy* and their subsequent engraving, were Blake's last great undertaking. Like so many projects of these years, they were the result of a commission by his younger fellow-artist John Linnell. The watercolours, of which 102 are recorded, were conceived in 1824. They are in varying stages of completion. While greatly admiring Dante's work, Blake characteristically felt that the mediaeval Italian's vision had shortcomings. He consequently incorporated revisions of the text in his designs (*plate 38*). This scene depicts an incident in the opening canto of the first book, *Hell*. Confronted by a lion, a wolf, and a leopard (who stand for the earthly powers that oppress him), Dante is rescued by the classical poet Virgil, who is to become his guide. As in all the other designs, Blake painted Dante in red to symbolize feeling, and Virgil in blue, symbolizing the superior quality of imagination.

Melbourne, National Gallery of Victoria

35. Dante and Virgil Penetrating the Forest

c.1824–6. Watercolour. 14$\frac{1}{2}$ × 20$\frac{3}{4}$in (37·1 × 52·7cm)

After having been rescued by Virgil, Dante asks the classical poet to guide him through the 'deep and wooded path' (*Hell*, II, 140). If, as has been suggested, the wood that they are penetrating consists of oak trees, then Blake may have been adding to their sinister overtones with his own interpretation. For in *Jerusalem* he associated oaks with the ancient druids, whom he condemned for their erroneous and savage religious practices. Only partially finished, this watercolour is one of the most lyrical of the Dante illustrations, the trees reinforcing the movement of the poets towards the fearsome dark beneath.

London, Tate Gallery

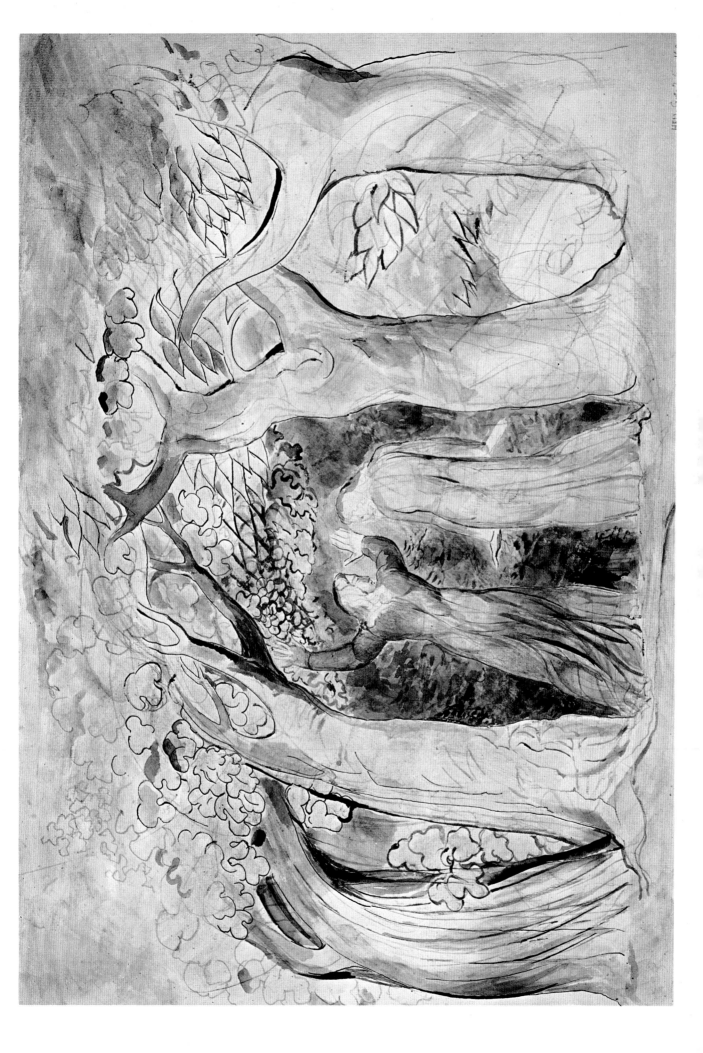

36. *The Inscription over the Gate*

c.1824–6. Watercolour. 20¾ × 14¾ in (52·7 × 37·4cm)

A depiction of the moment in Canto Three of *Hell* when
Dante and Virgil enter the gates of the infernal region. The
proverbial message above the portal – 'Abandon hope all
ye who enter here' – is written by Blake slightly
incorrectly in the original Italian and in his own
translation. In Blake's eyes the Hell described by Dante,
with all its oppression and legalistic divisions,
approximated most closely to the created material world. It
has been suggested that the four mounds, seen here
through the flaming opening, are intended to represent the
four major continents of this earth.

London, Tate Gallery

37. *The Circle of the Lustful – Paolo and Francesca*

c.1824–7. Watercolour. 14 × 20½in (37 × 52cm)

This is one of the most powerful and original of Blake's Dante illustrations. It depicts one of the incidents most favoured by the Romantics, the story, in Canto Five of *Hell*, of the ill-fated and adulterous lovers, Paolo and Francesca. Their punishment is to be borne eternally in a whirling, smiting wind with other sinful lovers in the second circle of Hell. Blake shows the moment when Paolo and Francesca are rejoining this whirlwind after having told their story to Dante. The Italian poet has meanwhile fainted.

Birmingham, City Museum and Art Gallery

38. *The Simoniac Pope*

1824–7. Watercolour. 20$\frac{3}{4}$ × 14$\frac{1}{2}$in (52·7 × 36·8cm)

A scene from Canto 19 of *Hell*, when Dante and Virgil are passing through the section of the eighth circle reserved for simoniacs (or corrupt clergy). The sinner plunged head downwards into the flames is Pope Nicholas III, whose fate is to remain so suspended until another pope, who has committed a similar sin, replaces him and pushes him deeper into the flames. At the top Virgil can be seen bearing Dante away after the interview. Blake has imaginatively made the opening in which the Pope is placed transparent so that his whole form can be seen. The red and blue that are dominant throughout all the Hell illustrations are alternated here to produce a flickering vibrancy of great effectiveness.

London, Tate Gallery

39. *Dante and Virgil Approaching the Angel who Guards the Entrance of Purgatory*

1824–7. Watercolour. 20¾ × 14½in (52·7 × 37·3cm)

In Canto 9 of *Purgatory* Dante and Virgil approach the angel who guards the gate of Purgatory. He is seated at the top of the three steps, representing sincerity, contrition, and love, that lead to the portal. The darkening sky, with the sun dramatically covered with clouds, fits in with the time of day described by Dante and serves to emphasize the brightness of the angel. It may also relate to Blake's criticism of Dante, which suggested that the latter's vision became less clear as he approached the more ethereal regions of Purgatory and Paradise.

London, Tate Gallery

40. *Beatrice Addressing Dante from the Car*

1824–7. Watercolour. 14½ × 20¾ in (37·2 × 52·7cm)

After having passed through Purgatory Dante encounters Beatrice, the woman whom he adored on earth who is now to guide him to Paradise. The car in which she appears is based on the description Dante gives in Canto 19 of Purgatory. In this the gryphon who pulls it symbolizes Christ, and Beatrice herself the Church. The girls in green, red and white are identifiable by their colours as, respectively, Hope, Charity and Faith. Certain alterations that Blake made to Dante's description suggest that he reinterpreted the theme to indicate the subjection of the poetic genius of Dante to the female will of Beatrice.

London, Tate Gallery

P.g. Canto 29 x 30

WILLIAM VAUGHAN AND BLACKER CALMANN COOPER LIMITED *would like to thank the following for allowing works in their collections to be reproduced in this book: the Brooklyn Museum, gift of William Augustus White (plate 19); Glasgow Art Gallery, Sterling Maxwell Collection (plates 22 and 23); Library of Congress, Rosenwald Collection (plates 4–6); the Museum of Fine Arts, Boston (plate 25); the National Trust of Great Britain (plates 23 and 24); the National Gallery of Victoria, Melbourne (plate 34); Princeton University Library (plate 7); the Tate Gallery, London (plates 2, 3, 11–14, 16, 21, 29, 32 and 35–40). Plates 1, 8, 9, 15, 26, 27, 30 and 33 are reproduced by permission of the Syndics of the Fitzwilliam Museum, Cambridge; plates 10 and 17 are reproduced by permission of the trustees of the British Museum; and plates 28 and 31 are reproduced by courtesy of the Trustees of the Pierpont Morgan Library. The Cooper-Bridgeman Library provided transparencies for plates 24 and 35; John Webb took the photographs for plates 3, 11, 13, 14, 16, 22, 32 and 38–40. Agnew's of London provided the transparency for plate 18.*